And What's Your Life's Drama?

Five Easy Steps
To Remove Drama From Your Life
And Set Your Soul Free...

Stelios Nicolaou

WHAT THIS TINY, HILARIOUS BOOK
CAN DO FOR YOU

The goal of this small book is to teach you a new, funny formula, the Woo-hoo Woo-hoo© method. This new formula will help you identify and neutralize dramatized thinking that often brings unnecessary drama, sorrow and misery in our lives. I am talking about helping you neutralize cloudy thoughts that do not come from the challenging circumstances themselves, but from unfulfilled dreams and aspirations.

By learning to apply the method described in this book, you will learn to defeat cloudy thoughts and develop a new thinking pattern that will eliminate drama from your life, setting your soul free.

I am Your Mistress, Your Drama Queen.
And You Are My Slave!

Now, let me introduce you to your escort.
Allow me now to introduce you to a fine lady who will be your guide
and keep you company in this book journey. Although she looks like a
dominant mistress holding a whip, please don't get scared or get
intimidated by her. Yes, at times, she can be very mean, loud,
bigheaded, angry, and controlling. Even so, appearances can be
deceiving.

She is not what she appears to be.
She is not what she appears to be. Soon you will discover that she is
not the enemy after all. When you get to know her, and when you
listen to what she has to say, she has many secrets to reveal and many
life-changing lessons to share. She will be your guide and will do the
talking from now on. I am sure that she will keep you a good company.
Have fun with her and don't forget to enjoy the journey.

I wish and pray for you to complete the book with a new perspective, a
new attitude, and a new way of thinking and inner freedom, so a
brand-new world will be revealed to you.

Sincerely,

The Author.

TABLE OF CONTENTS

DEDICATION

Dedicated to the reader who learns to let go of the past, the one who has the courage to forgive and forget, the one who is ready to do whatever it takes to make a difference in this world.

Chapter One
and What's the Root
of Your Life's Drama?

Understanding, Defining, and Naming
The Root of Your Life's Drama

And you are my slave.
I know who you are, slave. You are a submissive being, and I am your dominant Mistress and Drama Queen. You wish to follow my every command…You live to please me, I know.

You get what you deserve!
I allow you to be my unworthy slave, because you obey my every command. You are mine, and I like to punish and rule over you, in any way I can. I give you exactly what you deserve little worm.

Allow me to introduce myself, slave.
In this chapter I am going to explain to you who I am by giving you a good definition of my existence and identity. Once you learn who I really am, then I'll show you how you can name me… so I can be among the glamorous, the rich and the famous…

Why do you need to know me?
When you clarify in your mind your unique Miss Woo-hoo Woo-hoo, and when you personalize me by giving me an appropriate name, it will be a decisive, practical step toward understanding me, honoring me, so you can bow your knee before me, worship me and obey me as

your highness and master...

You have been my slave for many years!

I have news, slave! You are not a newly discovered slave of mine. I have been controlling you since many years now. You've been my obedient slave for a long time.

You need to know how I control you!

By identifying me with a unique name, you will begin to understand the way I influence and dominate you. Anyway, by giving me a name, you will end up understanding the ways I have been messing up your life.

**I am much more
than your dominant mistress and drama queen.**

The way I define myself is as follows:

Your Woo-hoo Woo-hoo is an image, person, relationship, memory, hope, or dream that still brings you intimacy, deep feelings of affection, love, romance, and closeness (warmth) of heart. Your personal Woo-hoo Woo-hoo is your strongest remembrance that could give or could have given meaning to the very existence of your being. Nonetheless, life, unfavorable circumstances and adversities refused to provide it, or may have taken it away from you.

Allow me to get more intimate, my dear.
I, your Personal Woo-hoo Woo-hoo could have been the memory of the loving mother or father that suddenly died or left you… I may have been the best-loved pet during your childhood…or a loving relationship with your soul mate, which for whatever reason ended unexpectedly…

I can also be the ideal career you were so passionate about, but you suddenly lost…, or I can be one of your greatest dreams that has never become real.

I am different from person to person.
I can be the loving relationship you've never experienced, or the one you've lost… I can be the key personal characteristic you think you are lacking… I can be a mental or a physical limitation you've carried with you since you were born… Or, I can be a desired goal such as a college degree, which for whatever reasons you couldn't earn…

I can have many faces.
I can also be the sudden loss of your loved one you were so depended on… or the loss of the job you really enjoyed. Similarly, I can be the longing for your dream career, or the longing for the ideal companion that would satisfy all your emotional and romantic needs.

I am still alive forever more…
You may not have realized or even remembered well what happened years ago. Nonetheless, your Drama Queen, Miss Woo-hoo Woo-hoo,

your Woo-hoo Woo-hoo, has been crystallized in time deep into your subconscious–becoming from conscious and specific to subconscious and vague. Yes! I am still inside you, although you probably don't even remember me anymore.

DEFINING MISS WOO-HOO WOO-HOO
AN EASIER, SHORTER DEFINITION

Your Personal Woo-hoo Woo-hoo is an object, a person, or relationship–any remembrance that brings deep feelings of love, affection, romance, and closeness (warmth) of heart, which you believed would have given meaning to the very existence of your being.

Here is a scientific definition of who I am.
I am the longings of unmet needs during your childhood years. I am
the wounded child in you that always wants, longs, cries, becomes
selfish, gets angry, and the child in you remains hurt, critical and
unsatisfied, because few of you humans have had a perfect childhood.

I am much more than your drama queen.
I am much more than a Drama Queen, or a dominant, mean Mistress. I
am your subconscious unwillingness to 'let go' of your Woo-hoo Woo-
hoo, creating a big hole and great void in your little heart.

I am your heart's greatest abyss.
Your unique Woo-hoo Woo-hoo goes much deeper than any ordinary
dream or goal as it is the big void created inside you, because of your
reluctance to "let go" of . . . that loving relationship you have lost . . . of
a key personal characteristic you think you are lacking . . . of a physical
limitation you may have . . . , or of a college degree (for whatever
reason) you could not earn.

Naming Your Personal Woo-hoo Woo-hoo.

Now that you have a good grasp of who Miss Woo-hoo Woo-hoo is,
let's discuss why giving me a name is so important.

Give me a name, pplease!
After you've realized who I am...that I am matchless, distinctive,
different and unique, I will allow you to go ahead and give me an
appropriate name. Hey, I have good intentions: One day, I want to be
one of the world's most glamorous bitches!

After all, I am your Mistress, slave.

After all I am your dominant Mistress, and you need to give me a name, so you can understand the unique influence and domination I have over you, your behavior and your life. (Yes, I love vanity. And that's why I would like you to give me a name, so I can continue to be selfish, big-headed and arrogant...)

Naming Me? What? Why?
By identifying and naming your personal Woo-hoo Woo-hoo, you transfer vague subconscious memories and feelings into the world of conscious existence–into your conscious mind–into reality–a place where I can be recognized, honored and praised for who I am.

Seriously, why naming me?
Once I have been identified, what's the benefit in taking the time to give a name to your Personal Miss Woo-hoo Woo-hoo?

Slave, I need a name to be real.
The answer is that your human brain needs to NAME something before it becomes REAL. Before something is named, it doesn't exist, because it is buried deep into your subconscious and your awareness of it is too dim. Or it doesn't exist, because you haven't noticed it or defined it yet. Consequently, you think that I might as well not be there.

You've buried me deep in your heart.
Although powerfully present in your everyday behavior, I was primarily formed during your childhood. Since many years have elapsed, I have been buried deep in your subconscious, changing form, from conscious and particular to a form that is now subconscious and vague.

So I can be recognized and honored!

By identifying me and by giving me an appropriate name, you'll transfer vague subconscious memories and feelings into the world of conscious existence–into your conscious mind–a place where I can be recognized, understood, and honored for what I am.

So, please set me free by giving me a name!
Anyway I am tired of remaining, vague and unknown, and buried in your past. I want you to recognize me for who I am. I want you to honor and … worship me, so I can breathe fresh air, feel alive, and be a proper bitch once again.

THIS IS HOW YOU CAN GIVE ME A RELEVANT NAME

Name me in a unique way.
I am the memory of the object, relationship, or person, which/who brings you deep feelings of affection, love, feelings of romance, closeness (warmth) of heart, triggering meaning to every fiber of your existence.

…Consequently, the NAME of your Woo-hoo Woo-hoo should instantly bring to mind those same feelings of warmth, feelings of closeness of heart…

Search for me, trace me, and name me.
The idea is to find a name that will connect you with your childhood–to connect you with the innocent and beautiful emotions you once felt when you were a child.

Although now you are a grown-up, you still have images, dreams and memories from your childhood, images that bring you intense feelings of intimacy that you once felt when you were a child.

Slave, give me a colorful, vibrant name.
Pick the strongest remembrance that brings such rich feelings of
emotions from your childhood–feelings derived from childhood that
are full of vibrancy, love, acceptance, hope, and understanding.

Then, all you have to do is give me a relevant name, so that each time
you recall my name, these human emotions of yours are aroused once
again.

I am not limited to your childhood years.
Although not limited to your childhood, memories and dreams of your
adulthood are built on your childhood experiences and therefore can
also arouse such profound intimate feelings. I could be your first
romantic love, the first kiss, or the unforgettable excitement you felt
from catching your first fish . . . or the first salary you got from your
first job.

Slave, I am your most vivid memory!
Such memories are embedded in your subconscious so deeply that
their recalling always triggers intense feelings of closeness and
intimacy. All you have to do is just choose the greatest of these
memories and subsequently give it a name.

I used to be innocent, romantic, and loving.
Go ahead and choose a name from the most cherished moments of
your life–even if it brings tears in your eyes. You may even imagine, or
dream a scene you always wanted to experience–then just label it with
the name of your choice.

Think with your head, although above all, think with your heart, when selecting the right name for your personal Woo-hoo Woo-hoo. A good idea is to go close to nature and test the name you have chosen.

The murmuring of the wind, and the soothing sound of the waves shall tell you if the name you have chosen is the right one.

Please give me a lovely, graceful name.
If the name is not simple, lovely, aligned with the simplicity, grace, and beauty of the trees, the sea, or the forest, and if it doesn't bring tears to your eyes, then change it and choose a name that it does. You see I used to be loving and innocent, a free spirit, beautiful and romantic. It's because you've buried me deep in your heart that I became a dominant Mistress, a bitch, arrogant, controlling, presumptuous and selfish.

Yes, slave,
I used to be innocent, beautiful and charming.

The name of my personal Woo-hoo Woo-hoo, the name that brings me intense memories and deep feelings of affection, feelings of romance, closeness and warmth of heart, the name that brings tears to my eyes is ______________(name it, slave!).

You've taken probably the most important step in the process of understanding my role in your life. Thanks! Now I have a name–now I feel alive and real. Slave, I thank you very much for...baptizing me.

Coming up Next: Chapter 2
What Your Drama is Doing To Your Life.

Chapter Two
What Your Drama
is Doing to Your Life

Because you are glued on me, your personal Woo-hoo Woo-hoo, you give me permission to flood your thinking with thoughts of fear, passivity, and insecurity as well as with thoughts of selfishness, cynicism, over ambition, unforgiveness, greed, vanity, and self-centeredness.

When I say you are my slave, I mean it.
When I say that you are enslaved to me, enslaved by your personal Miss Woo-hoo Woo-hoo, this is what I mean:

You are at my mercy, slave!
You are at the mercy of that person, relationship, memory, hope, (true or imaginary), that was supposed to bring you intimacy, deep feelings of affection, love, romance, and closeness of heart.

You are bonded and tied on the illusion of what life could have been, or what life could have given you.

You are hooked, needy on and–subconsciously–enslaved by the longings of your childhood.

You are tied to the past too much! As a result, you've become helpless to face reality and powerless to work on your future.

Slave, it's your fault, not mine!
You, yes it's YOU who allow me to rule over you, because you are at the mercy of that person, relationship, memory, hope, (true or imaginary), that would have brought you intimacy, deep feelings of affection, love, happiness, romance, and closeness of heart.

It's easy for me to be your control freak.
I easily control you because you are bonded and tied on the illusion of what life could have been, or what life could have given you...

It's your fault slave, not mine!

And you continue to be my slave ...
You are enslaved to me, your Woo-hoo Woo-hoo. You are tied to me, your personal Woo-hoo Woo-hoo, because you are not willing to let go of me, as you are always comparing your circumstances with what life

could have given you, with what you could have achieved.

Because you are fixed on your Woo-hoo Woo-hoo:

You do not have a healthy attachment with reality.

Your possibilities for better life seem limited.

Your inner freedom is partial and ineffective.

Your ability to make choices is damaged.

How I love twisting your reality, slave.
Because you are fixed on me, your illusory Woo-hoo Woo-hoo, you do
not enjoy a healthy understanding of now. Consequently, your choices
are limited, inner freedom is limited, and therefore your ability to
grow is weakened.

YOU ARE HOOKED AND ENSLAVED
BY THE LONGINGS OF YOUR CHILDHOOD.

Here is how I waste your life away...
I, your Woo-hoo Woo-hoo generate cloudy thoughts in your mind. As a
result, your heart reacts to such thoughts with feelings of fear,
passivity, insecurity, over ambition, selfishness, cynicism, vanity, or
egocentrism.

The Three Drama Plays.
In turn, I manage to dramatize your behavior. I dramatize your life by
enslaving you into one of the three main drama scripts: The 'Loser,' the
'Hunter,' and the 'Narcissist' drama plays.

Just don't deny it, slave.
When you are glued on me (your Miss Woo-hoo Woo-hoo) your sense of reality is like 'tunnel vision.' You are not in touch with reality. A limiting view of the world is what I your personal Woo-hoo Woo-hoo am bringing to your life.

You are bonded and tied on the illusion of what life could have been, or what life could have given you.

Because you are so much attached to your Woo-hoo Woo-hoo, you are unwilling to 'let go' of what you've always wanted in life.

As long as you remain attached on me, your Woo-hoo Woo-hoo, you continue to be in denial to accept what life has already given you–you refuse to accept reality for what it is.

Realize that it is the bond with me, your Woo-hoo Woo-hoo that compulsively pushes you to play strange drama plays that demoralizes you. It is the person, relationship, memory, hope, true or imaginary, that would have brought you intimacy, love, deep feelings of affection, romance, and closeness (warmth) of heart . . .that pushes you to over dramatize your life, because you are not willing to let go of your personal Woo-hoo Woo-hoo.

Slave, I am your destiny.
You are destined to act out a drama in life that is not yours, as it is a play alien to your personality and uniqueness. Regardless of what drama dominates your life, by living a dramatized life, you become my slave. You are in bondage because you are deprived the main ingredient of a healthy personality–inner freedom.

**Slave, how I love to make you
look desperate.**

Slave, your life's drama comes from despair.
In the next chapter, I will describe the three drama scripts you enact daily, in your attempt to fill the void in your heart, your reaction to fill the hole of your personal Woo-hoo Woo-hoo.

Because you won't let me go.
Because of your unwillingness to let me go, I will describe the three primary ways, how you respond to life, in your desperation to fill this void–the void of your personal Woo-hoo Woo-hoo, because you are

unwilling to let me go and carry on with your life.

Coming up Next: Chapter 3.
The Three Primary Dramas You Like to Play.

Chapter Three
The Three Primary Dramas
You Like to Play

I know how to push your buttons, slave!
Whether you've realized it or not, I, your Woo-hoo Woo-hoo, dominate your life. You may ask how in the world I manage to do just that? For me, it's simple. It's a piece of cake. I control and rule your life by pushing you to play one of the three dramas.

Let me explain it a little bit more.
While I remain untreated, I, your Woo-hoo Woo-hoo, create a big hole in your heart, which then I use it to trap you into one of the following, three drama scripts:

The Loser Drama Script

The Hunter Drama Script

The Narcissist Drama Script

So what are we waiting for, slave? Let's examine the first drama script, my popular one, 'The Loser' drama, which I use to control and ruin your life.

**Next: How I push you to play
The 'Loser' Drama.**

THE LOSER DRAMA SCRIPT

Trapping you into 'The Loser' Drama.
With my blessings, when I trap you into 'The Loser' drama, I provoke you to blame others and life because of your unfavorable circumstances. In this drama script, you habitually tend to complain about how unfairly life has treated you, and how unlucky you've been. I like it when you eventually adopt a victimized attitude, worsening your circumstances even more...

I make you feel victimized, powerless.
What I love about 'The Loser' drama play is that I make you feel victimized and powerless. And as a result, your victimized attitude prevents you from making choices that could improve your

circumstances right now. Ha ha ha!

You are forever mine, slave, when...
I trap you into this drama hole forever, when you are unwilling to
forgive others, and especially when you are not willing to forgive
yourself of what happened in the past and carry on with your life.

THIS IS HOW I MAKE YOU FEEL
IN 'THE LOSER' DRAMA.

By trapping you into 'The Loser' drama play, I make you feel shy,
lonely, reactive, critical, and hypersensitive. Moreover, when I trap you
into 'The Loser' drama play, I make you unforgiving, rebellious,
complaining and blaming people and circumstances of how unfair life
is and how others have mistreated you.

Slave, life doesn't owe you a thing!
In this drama script, you hold the belief that you are entitled to
receiving all the best life could give. You also think that life owes you
happiness. You've adopted the false conviction that 'It was life's
responsibility' to make you happy...

Said in a different way, you believe that it was life's obligation to
satisfy you with your Woo-hoo Woo-hoo, (that image, person,
relationship, remembrance, hope, or dream that would have brought
intimacy, deep feelings of affection, romance, satisfaction, and warmth
in your heart...)

"They Took My Woo-hoo Woo-hoo
Away From Me."

It's the "They took my Woo-hoo Woo-hoo away from me" belief and
attitude that activates 'The Loser' drama script. You adopt the
conviction that life has deprived you of something very important that
could have made you fulfilled and happy.

Next, I will describe the second drama play, I use to torment you: 'The
Hunter' Drama.

**Next: How I trap you into
'The Hunter' Drama Play.**

Hunting for your Woo-hoo Woo-hoo Illusion.
Just as a hunter who loves hunting for the sake of it, once I trap you in this drama script, you constantly pursue more and more goals, as the previously-attained goal was not enough to bring you satisfaction and peace. Whether the goal was about a new career, a vacation, a new house, or any other material possession, it has not filled the void created by me (your Woo-hoo Woo-hoo).

And here is how I poison your life.
The way I rule over your life, using 'The Hunter' drama script, is by poisoning you with a lack of contentment. As I manage to persuade you that I am missing from your life, you repeatedly set higher and higher goals to get me. Once the goal is achieved, you go for the next goal, hoping that 'this time' you will find the peace, joy, and satisfaction that you seek.

Ensnaring you into 'The Hunter' Drama.
Whether it's about career goals, relationships, or social status aspirations, every time I trap you in to 'The Hunter' drama script, you think that you know what you want 'this time' and surely know how to get it. You hope that reaching your new goal will bring true happiness and contentment that will fill the void in your heart.

You will get me this time, or so you think.
This time, you think, you will hunt down what is missing in your life, which would bring you true happiness, "intimacy, deep feelings of affection, romance, and warmth of heart ..."

This is the way I whip your head, slave.

I whip your head by flooding you with a constant demands and requests, commanding you to go for the next girlfriend or boyfriend, for a bigger house, the next job promotion or for the next material possession, hoping that this time the next goal, the next achievement, will be the one you were looking for all your life.

I am sucking joy out of you, slave!
My little slave, just like a vampire, I love sucking joy out of your life! I fancy when I steal precious moments from you, as by trapping you into 'The Hunter' drama play, I make you incapable of appreciating and tasting the simple things and pleasures of life. When I trap you into 'The Hunter' drama play, you tend to be eager, anxious, as you have not learned how to slow down and be at peace with yourself.

And here is how I do it.
You may not realize it, nonetheless, I am sucking out simple joys from your life, when you forget to smell the roses, when you don't give frequent hugs to your children, when you forget to connect with others and with God.

Next: How I trap you into
the 'Narcissist' Drama Play.

The 'Narcissist' Drama Script

Whether serving a passionate career, relationship, a hobby, or any other activity, the way I trap you into 'The Narcissist' drama play is by letting your passion for a single aspect of your life to consume you.

'Finding' Heaven on planet Earth.
I trap you into this drama script, when you become infatuated by a single activity, when your passion for it overshadows everything else in your life–when you think you've found Heaven on planet Earth.

Tricking you into a golden cage.
Whether your passion is for a hot relationship, a promising career, a hobby, or for any other type of activity that brings temporary infatuation, I manage to give you the impression that you've made it in life, that you have it all...that you have found your Woo-hoo Woo-hoo at last.

I become your idol, your goddess.
The little utopia world in which you people of this drama manage to trap yourselves in is the only activity that gives meaning to your life. Eventually your passion becomes an idol, a 'god,' an object you passionately value... and worship.

Self-imprisoned in your little, golden cage.
At the end, the way I trap you into 'The Narcissist' drama play grows to be so self-consuming that you become indifferent of what's going on beyond your 'little world.' In essence, you've created and live in a little, golden cage that has become your obsession, an object of worship–nonetheless, a prison.

The concern is that persons who operate in this drama script develop such a consuming passion for a particular activity, career, or relationship that they ignore the other roles they have to play in life.

Slave, can't you see, the stakes are high?
Engaging in this type of drama script costs you too much, though at first you don't realize the high price you will have to pay. Your passion becomes your obsession. It becomes your primary affection, so everything else in your life orbits around it, with less priority and significance. You are consumed by your obsession, so as what you do is all what you are–your passion is the only role you play and the only activity that gives meaning and identity in your life.

The rest of life's roles, either have low importance or serve to support and perpetuate this meaningless, drama.

Slave, it's a subtle, and dangerous drama.
Although it may not be a so obvious drama in people when compared with 'The Loser' and 'The Hunter' drama plays, 'The Narcissist' drama play is by far the most subtle and dangerous. That's why I love it so much.

You lose sight of life's direction.
Whenever I trap you in this drama script, you become so consumed by your high-in-demand talent, relationship, or other passionate activity that you become self-absorbed and self-centered. As a result, you end up living an unbalanced life, unaware of where you are heading.

You don't realize it until it's too late.
And the best part of it is that when your little, utopia castle goes through a sudden demolition, when your little utopia for whatever reason collapses, you crumble with it as well!

Don't wait until it's too late, slave!
Until it is too late, you become so deeply self-absorbed in your little, utopian world that you rarely realize that something may be wrong with the other roles you have to play.

The fate of 'The Narcissist' Drama.
Good examples of the fate of this drama are corporate executives who jump out of the window because their business is ruined, as well as ordinary people who just cannot recover from the loss of a significant relationship. Both of them decide to end their lives, because their passion for it was the only 'life' they knew.

Slave, aren't you sacrificing too much?
Although there is nothing wrong with living a passionate life, 'The Narcissist' drama script kicks in, nonetheless, when one role in your life dominates and overshadows the other roles. Moreover, all other roles in your life such as spouse, parent, etc, become tools to support the hobby, person, activity, relationship, or job that resembles so much with your Woo-hoo Woo-hoo. Many times, the other roles in your life become necessary sacrifices to support your narcissistic, egotistic, self-consuming behavior.

Again, it's not really my fault.
Listen to me slave. It's not my fault when you allow ONE PASSION in life to consume and dominate you.

Having a passion for life, a passion for your career, or passion for a relationship is not wrong. It becomes risky and self-destructive, nevertheless, when you allow it to overshadow everything else in your life.

Coming up Next: Chapter 4
What the three drama plays have in common.

Chapter Four
What The Three Dramas
Have In Common?

The first drama script, 'The Loser', describes people who have lost hope in life. They think they've lost all hope to satisfy and fill the void created by their personal Miss Woo-hoo Woo-hoo. People acting out the second play, 'The Hunter' drama, endlessly chase and pursue activities to fill the void of their Woo-hoo Woo-hoo. The third drama script, 'The Narcissist' describes persons who think they've satisfied the void created by their Woo-hoo Woo-hoo.

Slave, all three are just an illusion.
What people in the three drama scripts have in common is that they act on an illusion. While the first drama, 'The Loser', portrays people who experience a lack of the illusion of their Woo-hoo Woo-hoo, people trapped in the second drama, 'The Hunter', chase after the illusion of their Woo-hoo Woo-hoo. The third drama play, 'The Narcissist', describes people living in an illusion of their Woo-hoo Woo-hoo (they think the void of their Woo-hoo Woo-hoo is satisfied by the temporary passion they pursue).

So, What's Your Favorite Drama?
Regardless of what drama you play, you are not in control. I am the one who holds the whip. I am the one who is controlling you, slave. While you remain in bondage with me, you will continue to be my submissive bondman.

Slave, allow me to explain.

Daily, you may enact all the three drama scripts interchangeably. Nonetheless, there is a main drama script of the three that drives and dominates your behavior and therefore your life.

So what's your favorite drama?

So, what's your favorite drama play?
Which one of the three drama scripts, I, your personal Woo-hoo Woo-hoo, motivate you to play unwillingly and compulsively?

IDENTIFY YOUR SELF!
ARE YOU A HUNTER, A LOSER, OR A NARCISSIST?

Are you a never-satisfied Hunter, or a Narcissist–a Self-consumed, seemingly content and successful person? Or are you a Loser, who thinks that has lost all hope?

Although in daily life, I manage to enslave you to enact the three principal drama scripts alternatively, there is a primary drama play that drives and dominates your behavior over the long run.

Slave, acting out a drama is self-limiting.
Any of the three principal drama scripts exhibits an enslaved individual. Such persons are glued on their Miss Woo-hoo Woo-hoo. They are 'fixed' on their personal Woo-hoo Woo-hoo. ...And you will continue to be in bondage with me. And I will continue to be your dominant mistress, controlling and directing your life.

Enacting a drama is a no laughing matter!
Because of the vainness of the three main drama scripts, people trapped in any one of them become dependent personalities–they are individuals who are at high risk to suffer from identity crisis, nervous breakdown and other devastating consequences.

Learn to deal with me slave, or else...
Until you learn to identify me and neutralize me in your thinking, you are doomed to fall into the trap of the three principal drama scripts, I love to trap you in–so I can continue to torture, demoralize, and bring you grief and misery.

When you engage in one of the three drama scripts, you become my slave. You behave in a manner that is not you, your way, your authentic self, your mission, your purpose in life.

Every time I enslave you to enact any of the three drama plays, I weaken your inner freedom. I limit in this way your choices that could improve and bring meaning in your life.

 With the three drama scripts controlling your life, I prevent you from living life to the fullest. You have no idea how much I love it when it happens, slave. Ha, ha, ha.

Coming up Next: Chapter 5
'Cause you don't really need drama.

CHAPTER FIVE
BECAUSE YOU DON'T
REALLY NEED DRAMA

SET ME FREE WHY DON'T YOU BABE?

You just don't need me.
And because I want to prove to you that once upon a time I was innocent and charming, and not the bitch you brought me up to become, I will give you some advice that bitches and freaks don't usually give to their victims.

Can you keep a secret?
(But pplease keep it between us as (B&FI) the Bitches and Freaks International may find out and expel me from their organization!).

And the secret I want to tell you is..
You don't really need me, because you are an awesome person. Yes, you've heard me right: You are beautifully and wonderfully made.

Gold is in Your genes!
The truth about you is that you don't really need me. Your worth is beyond your unmet needs and unfulfilled dreams. You are greater than your circumstances, no matter how sorrowful or painful they seem. Your worth is greater than your feelings, beyond your behavior, more valuable than your heredity, or who you currently perceive yourself to be. You are more valuable from any talents and other good qualities that you think you are lacking.

You are truly priceless and unique.
Your feelings, behavior, and talents describe just a dimension of who you are–just one part of you–as you are much more mysterious, multidimensional and multifaceted than any given definition, because of your human nature, your human origin.

Your brain is more valuable than the universe.
Science now tells us that the human brain's structure and composition is much more complex than the stars and galaxies in the known universe.

I have to confess, you are a sacred being!

Slave, Forget Psychology and Medicine!
Yes, you've heard me right! Forget about how medicine, psychology and science may attempt to define you. No science can correctly define your worth and your uniqueness. Whatever definition science or medicine may give you, it is not you! Their definition is incomplete. Modern psychology, or any other science, cannot shrink you to one of their convenient 'labels,' as science can see just one part of you–not the whole, multidimensional person you truly are.

Your Worth is Always Greater..
You are more than a category or a label they
try to put you in, because science' DEFINITION
is RELATIVE and therefore PARTIAL, and
consequently LIMITED. Science' relative
knowledge can define just a part of you, not the
whole person, multidimensional, eternal soul,
you truly are.

Even in the middle of challenging circumstances, your uniqueness is rare, incomparable and eternal just because you are a human being–of divine origin and eternal value.

You are beautiful even when in error.
Don't you know that you are beautiful even in the way you make mistakes? No other species has this attribute. You are matchless, you are an awesome, mysterious, sacred being–you are mysteriously and magnificently unique–even when in error!

You are matchless, even in your tragedies.
You are inexplicably amazing even in the middle of your tragedies! In fact, the story of your life could write a tragedy much more amazing than the writings of Euripides, Sophocles, or even Shakespeare. You could be a person much more dramatic than Antigone. You are a remarkable being, indeed!

Your pain is also beyond compare.
Even in the middle of tragic circumstances, you are exceptional. You may be in pain right now. Your pain is also unparalleled–it is singular to you.

If you remain open to your struggles..
Nonetheless, if you remain open to your struggle, the soreness that you go through right now will be the door and catalyst for acquiring a new awareness of who you are. It will create in you a new insight of who you truly are. It will empower you to make a difference in your world.

You will never be the same again!
Your pain will become the tool for a life-searching and life-changing experience! What you go through now, will motivate you to discover dimensions of yourself and talents you never thought you had. The positive side of suffering is what makes you rethink about the things that matter. Pain makes you redefine who you are. Struggle and pain will motivate you to reevaluate where you are heading in life.

Adopt the right attitude.
Difficult circumstances, pain, and agony, many times pressure you to reevaluate your relations with others, resulting in better, happier relationships–more aligned with the universal principles of life and human conduct.

With the right attitude, you will be empowered to *rediscover* and *reinvent* yourself. If you humbly accept and collaborate with your challenging circumstances and suffering, you will end up creating a new life with meaning and purpose.

So let me go, slave!

SHAKING OFF YOUR PERSONAL WOO-HOO WOO-HOO

Say goodbye to old dreams and aspirations.
Childhood dreams and desires are valuable and important as they have something worthy to teach you. Nonetheless, as you travel through the journey of life, your values and priorities inevitably evolve and change. What was important to you then, when you were younger, is no longer important now.

When your dreams and your current values are no longer in agreement, it's time to think about rediscovering, reshaping and renewing your dreams, by giving them a new name, adopting a new purpose and a new direction.

It's time to say goodbye to me, after all.
Old dreams and obsolete desires and aspirations and other woo-hoos woo-hoos just don't make sense now. The way you find meaning in life has changed for good. I don't seem to represent anything meaningful to you anymore slave, as I belong to the past. The reason I exist is because you are not willing to let me go!

Slave, it's time to kiss me goodbye!
So kiss me goodbye and instead, use the innocence, and the wonder you once felt when you were a child to start dreaming again. Recreate and redefine your dreams once more, and embark on a journey with new mission and destination. So get over me slave, and go on with your life, and sail for new lands and new victories, in the world of endless possibilities.

GO AHEAD AND RELEASE ME BABE
'CAUSE YOU DON'T REALLY LOVE ME…

You don't really need me,

set me free, why don't you babe?

Allow me to get out of your life,

why don't you babe?

'cause you don't really need me,

you just let me keep you hangin' on!

You don't really need me,

'cause you just let me keep you hangin' on!

Why do you keep on coming around me,

playing with and torturing your own heart?

Why don't you get me out of your life

so that you can make a new start?

Get over me babe,

the way I've got over you..

Down deep you thing you still miss me,

but your heart and soul needs to be free,

If you wish to set yourself free,

you don't wanna still hold on me!

'cause I don't care a thing about you,

I am just using you!

Go ahead and get me out of your life,

so you can sleep at night,

'cause you don't really need me,

You just want me to keep you hanging' on....

You Keep Me Hangin' On
Diana Ross and the Supremes Lyrics ©
(paraphrase mine)

Coming up Next: Chapter 6
Sorting out The Root of Your Life's Drama!

CHAPTER SIX
SORTING OUT THE ROOT
OF YOUR LIFE'S DRAMA

Taking the first step.

Before I will go on and explain you the 'Five Easy Steps' how to *dedramatize* your thoughts and remove drama from your life, why don't you take the very first step–the introductory step–that sets the foundation of the Woo-hoo Woo-hoo method. This step is no other than NICKNAMING your personal Woo-hoo Woo-hoo.

Nicknaming me? What??

Do you remember when I asked you to give me a name (chapter one)? And you've honored my request and you've given me a name that represents your own, personal Miss Woo-hoo Woo-hoo. Your Woo-hoo Woo-hoo name symbolizes something very precious to you. I believe that you've given the best name to represent Me–your personal Woo-hoo Woo-hoo and Mistress.

It's ok to cry over my shoulder, slave.

In fact, if you did a good job, the name you've given me is supposed not only to excite your memory and emotions of the very things you used to love, but also to bring tears to your eyes–of what life could have been, of what life could have given you, or of what life for no apparent reason has taken away from you.

Slave, it felt so good!

Giving me a name was a great step in the process of *dedramatizing* your life. The moment you gave me a name, I felt great! You have no idea how it felt to be alive and breathe fresh air once again. Now that I have a name, I feel real, genuine and alive. Thank you very much for baptizing me and for giving me a name.

All I want now is to give me a nickname.
Well this time I am going to ask you to make yourself another favor. This time I am going to ask you to nickname Me. Yes slave. You've heard it right. I want you to NICKNAME your personal Woo-hoo Woo-hoo.

Take the next step, slave.
So what are you waiting for, slave? All you have to do is to convert your Woo-hoo Woo-hoo name into a nickname. Therefore, take the next step, you little worm, and just nickname me. Remember, people may forget a name. But who can easily forget a nickname?

Why am I asking you to nickname me?
Here is the answer to your question: The funnier the NICKNAME you'll choose for your Woo-hoo Woo-hoo, the greater will be your ability to neutralize dramatized thinking and respective dramatized behavior that makes your life miserable.

Naming me wasn't enough.
Just wanted to remind you that dramatized thinking is generated by your personal Miss Woo-hoo Woo-hoo...generated by that precious object, person, or dream, of what life would have given you, or of what life has taken away from you. By getting me a NICKNAME, you make me sound less serious and dramatic. With just the NAME you've given me, you've made me look like a drama queen. And slave, who wants to be a drama queen anyway?

Nicknaming Me is the key to *de-dramatization.*

Affirmative, slave. By nicknaming me, you convert your personal Woo-hoo Woo-hoo in to something cute, and funny–in to a name that can make you smile, instead of bringing tears to your eyes…and crying over my shoulders… of what life would have been … of what life could have given you….

Let's make a deal.
From now on, I take an oath: The funnier the NICKNAME you will choose for me, the less drama I will radiate over your life. The more hilarious and funny the nickname you will give me, the less trouble I will bring in your life. Agree? Yes? Do we have a deal?

HINTS ON NICKNAMING YOUR WOO-HOO WOO-HOO.

A good idea to find the right Nickname is to search for cute, funny names on the internet. Search for adorable baby names, dog names, or even cute cat names.

More hints in selecting the right nickname.

Use your imagination to come up with a nickname that is short and fun.

Then, convert it by breaking it into a <u>two-syllable</u> name and repeat it to add extra fun!

Slave, here is an example.
Let me give you an example: If the Woo-hoo Woo-hoo name you've chosen is Natalie, then you can nickname it by converting it to Nat-ta, or Na-ti-ta, Na-tie, or simply Na-ti Na-ta

If your Woo-hoo Woo-hoo name is Melissa, a cute, funny Nickname can
be Missy or Missy-missy, or even Missy-miss.

Here is the author's example:
Woohoo has been the author's remembrance, describing his emotions
after catching his first fish. He still remembers the awesomeness, the
wonder, the wow, and the thrill he felt after he caught his first fish,
back then, when he was six years old. Woohoo is the name he has
chosen to connect himself with his childhood, cherishing the awesome
memories, when life was so wonderful, carefree, joyful…magical,
playful, full of wonder.

He named me 'Woohoo'.
So he named ME 'Woohoo'. If you look it up in the dictionary Woohoo
is defined as an exclamation of joy, approval, etc. It's an "Expression of
excitement" used to convey exuberant, sudden joy delight or approval.

It reminds him the wonder and the wow!
The name Woohoo symbolizes the innocence, the wonder, and the
wow of his childhood. He often recalls his childhood years that were
full of magical adventure, with no stress, and no responsibilities. Every
day was a new day, a new opportunity to wonder, have fun, play and
explore.

And he nicknamed me 'Woo-hoo Woo-hoo'.
Woohoo is the name that still brings tears in the eyes of the author.
Nonetheless, after he has nicknamed me, changing and converting my
name FROM 'Woohoo!' TO 'Woo-hoo Woo-hoo', now he smiles and
sometimes he laughs whenever he recalls my name or when he
remembers me.

And the way he decided to nickname me was to call me Woo-hoo Woo-
hoo. In other words, he broke down the 'Woohoo' name to two-word

disyllables name: Woo-hoo Woo-hoo. You can convert your name in this way too.

Do it, slave. Nickname me, please!
Please go ahead and give me a nickname right now, so I can become funny, care free, and playful. I don't want to remain a drama queen. By nicknaming me, you'll make me feel as if I am a butterfly instead of the little, ugly freak imprisoned in the hidden dungeon of your heart.

If you don't nickname me, then..
If you don't nickname me, I am warning you slave. I know where you live! I will come to you and whip your head and keep on trapping you into the three miserable drama scripts of 'The Hunter',' The Loser', and 'The Narcissist.' You will continue to be mine, and I will continue to punish and rule over you without mercy. I'll give you exactly what you deserve little worm. And I will not let you go until you give me a nice, cute, little funny, hilarious nickname. Am I asking for too much?

**Slave, I will not let you go until
you give it to me.**

Once you give me a Nickname, write it down:

Your Personal Woo-hoo Woo-hoo Nickname Declaration

____

The Nickname of my Personal Woo-hoo Woo-hoo is the following:

My Woo-hoo Woo-hoo NICKNAME is

_______________.

____

Coming up next: Chapter 7

I will describe and explain in detail the Five Easy Steps that will *dedramatize* your soul. I will explain in detail, how to use the five-step method to recognize and neutralize cloudy, dramatic thoughts one thought at a time. So slave, what are you waiting for? Let's go!

Coming up Next: Chapter 7
Removing Drama from Your Life

Chapter Seven
Removing Drama from Your Life
In Five Easy Steps

Five easy Steps to Remove Drama From Your Soul and Set Your Mind Free

Slave, it's easier than you think.
Dedramatizing, or removing drama from your life, is easier than you think. Reaching emotional freedom by learning to *dedramatize* your soul may sound sophisticated and complex. I assure you that neither complex NLP techniques are involved, nor bizarre principles of parapsychology are used. *Dedramatization* is simple and straightforward. Applying the method of this little book is as simple as counting with your five fingers. All you have to know is the NICKNAME of your Woo-hoo Woo-hoo and the three chief drama plays I use to trap you in.

Before proceeding, please review:
-The meaning of your personal Woo-hoo Woo-hoo.
-Your Woo-hoo Woo-hoo NAME and NICKNAME.
-The three major dramas I love to trap you in.
-The main drama you tend to play in Life.

Study and get to know me once again.
It is essential to have a crystal-clear understanding of who I am. What I, Miss Woo-hoo Woo-hoo means personally to you, and how I influence your thinking. Likewise, make sure you understand the three principal drama scripts, I push you to play in your everyday life.

Dedramatizing **one thought at a time.**
By applying the simple, Five-step Method that follows, you will be able to recognize dramatized thoughts easily and provide the appropriate remedy 'on the fly!' Next, you will learn to correct dramatized thinking by shifting your thoughts from negative to neutral, and in doing so, setting your soul free from the enslaving power of Miss Woo-hoo Woo-hoo.

FIVE-STEPS TO INNER FREEDOM
A BRIEF SUMMARY OF THE FIVE-STEP METHOD©

1. Detect, Recognize, and Pause.
Listen, detect and identify dramatized thinking, and then make a mental pause.

2. Recognize it's Me Again.
Become aware and recognize it is I, Miss Woo-hoo Woo-hoo behind dramatized thinking. Slave, it's your Woo-hoo Woo-hoo behind the scenes.

3. Name Cloudy Thinking after My Nickname.
Name, tag and label those dramatized thoughts after your Woo-hoo Woo-hoo nickname.

4. Watch Out For The Three Drama Scripts.
Detect and become aware what particular drama script your personal Woo-hoo Woo-hoo is pushing you to play.

5. Now You Can Choose!

Exercise your freedom. Take an alternative action free from the power of the drama script you are about to play.

And now the Five Step Method© in full detail.

Five-steps to Emotional Freedom

Step One
Identify Dramatized Thinking
and then make a mental Pause

Pay Attention and Listen!
It's easy to recognize emotionally charged, over dramatized thoughts as they give you a 'gut feeling' that something is wrong. Something in your thinking and feelings just doesn't feel right.

Detect your immediate action.
Another way to identify dramatized thinking is by observing what action such thoughts motivate you to take. If such thoughts motivate you to play one of the three drama scripts, then it is thinking that is over dramatized.

Make a mental Pause.
Once you've identified dramatized thoughts in your thinking, just stop! Consciously make a pause. Take a mental time-out. Just be patient with dramatized thoughts. Resist the temptation to respond reactively to them. This is the reactive nature of dramatized thinking you try to correct.

Say, 'Wait a minute!'
Make a pause of the stream of thoughts, by saying to yourself, "Wait a minute!" or "just a second!" Take a few deep breaths to release tension. In this way, you avoid becoming reactive to dramatized thinking.

Don't take it seriously, slave.
By reacting too fast, you may take too seriously what your dramatized thoughts are saying. Remember, you don't take dramatized thoughts seriously or rationally, despite how convincing or dramatic they may appear. Such thoughts may look as if they are realistic, sensible, logical and urgent. Nevertheless, their purpose is to trap you into one of the three drama plays.

Step 2: Slave, it's me again!

STEP TWO
REALIZE IT'S ME AGAIN!

Realize It's me, your Woo-hoo Woo-hoo who generates such thoughts. Acknowledge that it is I, Miss Woo-hoo Woo-hoo, who is behind the dramatized thoughts you've just thought.

Slave, it is your Mistress behind the scenes.
Yes, I am the one behind every dramatized thought of yours. Thoughts of fear, passivity and insecurity as well as thoughts of selfishness, unforgiveness, cynicism, over ambition, greed, vanity, and self-centeredness don't come from you. It's neither your mind who generates such thoughts, nor your circumstances no matter how bad they seem to be.

Slave, it is I who is fooling you.
It is I, your personal Woo-hoo Woo-hoo, who is fooling you, by flooding your soul with such ugly thoughts as you are still subconsciously (attached) glued on me. After all, what did you expect after locking me in the darkest dungeon of your heart for such a long time?

STEP THREE
NAME THOSE DRAMATIZED THOUGHTS
AFTER YOUR WOO-HOO WOO-HOO NICKNAME.

In order to understand where your dramatized thoughts are coming from, NAME them after your personal Woo-hoo Woo-hoo Nickname.

Nickname those cloudy thoughts.
Say to yourself, "Oh It's my Woo-hoo Woo-hoo again!" In this way you've just categorized dramatized thoughts, and therefore you can begin to marginalize them away from your mind. By labeling them with your personal Woo-hoo Woo-hoo NICKNAME, it's just like you've put such cloudy thinking into a box at the back of your mind.

Nickname it to neutralize it!
By naming dramatized thinking after your Woo-hoo Woo-hoo NICKNAME, the power of such thoughts...comes to the surface and ceases to be mysterious, confusing, and dangerous. Such catastrophic, dramatic thinking is *dedramatized*. Its destructive burden over you, therefore, is neutralized. Instead of being serious and dramatic, your thinking now becomes calm, relaxed, sweet, and funny.

Step 4: Slave, watch out!

STEP FOUR
WATCH OUT FOR THE THREE DRAMA SCRIPTS!

Watch out for my drama script.
Look out for what drama script I am pushing you to play. Once you realize that it is I, Miss Woo-hoo Woo-hoo, who is rooted in dramatized thinking, causing you to think dramatized, self-destructive thoughts, keep your eyes open and watch out for what drama your

Woo-hoo Woo-hoo is about to push you to play.

Stop, ponder, and look out..
Stop, ponder, and look out what drama play you are about to enact
because of such emotionally charged thoughts. I remind you again that
such emotionally charged, cloudy thoughts may look as if they are
realistic, sensible and rational. Do not be deceived, though. Their
purpose is to entangle you and trap you into one of the three
demoralizing drama scripts: 'The Loser' drama play, 'The Hunter'
drama play, or 'The Narcissist' Drama. Slave, Watch out!

Reacting is for animals, slave.
It's easy to become over reacting and act upon your emotions,
especially when emotions are hot and boiling. However, by reacting to
dramatized thoughts is the same as choosing to play one of the three
dramas. Remember, animals do not think–they just react to their
environment and surroundings. You humans, on the other hand, after
observing you for some time, you have the ability to think and plan
ahead before acting.

You're smarter than your circumstances.
 You have the ability to imagine different paths of action other than
what your emotions are telling you. Simply said, your species is
smarter than your circumstances. You are also smarter than your
emotions. You have the rare ability to make a plan and follow a
strategy other than what your circumstances or what your emotions
are commanding you.

Reacting can be dangerous.
By over reacting, you fall in the trap of one of the three drama scripts
that unnecessarily over dramatize your life and drive you away from
living a life with purpose, mission and authenticity. Reacting can be

very dangerous, slave.

Reminding you of this, slave.
Your drama script detaches you from reality. It is blindly guiding you
to a destination that has nothing to do with the real you, who you are,
where you want to go, and where your happiness really is. It drives
you away from freedom and happiness.

Step 5: Now you can choose!

STEP FIVE
NOW YOU CAN CHOOSE!

Slave, now you can choose.
Now you have the right mindset to make a free choice. Now that you
know all the facts, exercise your free will and command yourself to
stop enacting such an unhealthy drama script. Exercise your Inner
Freedom to halt the playing the game of the three dramas. Say to
yourself, 'Game over Miss Woo-hoo Woo-hoo'.

Say it, slave!
Say, "Game over to 'The Loser' drama play". "Game over to 'The Hunter' drama game". "Game over to 'The Narcissist' drama script". Say, "Game over Miss Woo-hoo Woo-hoo!" Say, "I can choose another path". "I can choose my path, my way. "I can choose what I truly want, away from the three drama plays that confuse and misguide me".

Now you have enough freedom to choose.
"Between stimulus and response there is a space," according to Stephen Covey, who wrote the book, "The seven habits of highly effective people." You are now becoming aware that the Stimulus is your personal Miss Woo-hoo Woo-hoo and the cloudy, dramatized thoughts she generates. The Response–if you choose hastily to react to such dramatized thoughts–will be no other than giving in and allowing yourself to be trapped in one of her three drama scripts.

Exercise your uniqueness.
Remember the difference between your species and the animal kingdom. Animals react to their circumstances. You humans are different. You have the ability to respond intelligently. You can pro act. You have the freedom to choose how to respond to your circumstances, despite how tragic and enslaving they seem to be.

Now you can choose differently!
Now that you have created inner freedom by becoming aware of your Woo-hoo Woo-hoo, the dramatized thoughts she generates, and the three self-destructive drama scripts she tries to trap you in, you are empowered to decide differently. You can act away from the three destructive drama scripts. You've created enough freedom that enables you to choose the correct path aligned with your genuine needs, true mission, life purpose, and destination. Go ahead and make a decisive choice, consistent with your authentic self, where all your genuine needs can be met.

Learning to recognize emotionally charged thoughts (at any given moment) and naming them after the NICKNAME of your Woo-hoo Woo-hoo, as well as detecting what drama script such thoughts motivate you to play, you are shifting your emotions from Woo-hoo Woo-hoo dependent to Woo-hoo Woo-hoo independent thinking–free thinking that brings about clarity and freedom.

Slave, now you are free.

By detecting what drama script your personal Woo-hoo Woo-hoo is ready to trap you in, you detach yourself from the power of emotional, clouded thinking and the power your Woo-hoo Woo-hoo. You are set free from your personal Miss Woo-hoo Woo-hoo. By following and applying the Five-Step© Method, you are becoming Woo-hoo Woo-hoo free.

**Coming up Next: Chapter 8
Dealing with the Spiritual Side
of Your Life's Drama.**

Chapter Eight
Dealing With The Spiritual Side
Of Your Life's Drama

Giving you the KEY to freedom.
It would have been easy for me if I was to exclude from this book the chapter on spirituality. Why is that slave? Because giving you the KEY to genuine spirituality, it hurts me too much! The KEY seriously threatens my power, dominion and control over you. I won't be able to torture you anymore you little worm, and that sucks!

But... do you really want it?
 You see, if I give you the KEY to true spirituality, it will bring you freedom. It will set you free for good. It will liberate you from me once and for all. To be honest, I haven't decided if I really want to set you free yet. Besides, are you willing to receive the KEY? The KEY is free, just like any gift. Although it's free, still you must be willing to receive it. Believe me, many folks like you, for some strange reasons, just don't want it. They want to continue to live in bondage. What about you? Do you really want it?

Do you really want the KEY?

Who wants to be with you anyway?

Whether you want the KEY or not, I have to admit that ruling over you and bringing misery in your life does not fascinate me anymore. Allowing you to be my unworthy slave just doesn't bring me pleasure and excitement any longer. Besides, who wants to continue to control a miserable, pathetic human such as you? Nope! Not I. Not anymore, slave.

Anyway, after teaching you the Five-Step© method, you've learned how to neutralize dramatized thoughts, and now you know how to avoid the snare of the three drama plays. In this way, I have to admit that my authority, power and control over you are not as strong as they used to be. As you habitually neutralize drama in your thinking, my control over you becomes weaker day by day. Hmm.. I guess, it's time for me to leave.

So get rid of me, slave.

Besides, I want to get away from you as well. And I will tell you everything you need to know that will help me escape from the dark dungeon you've locked me in for such a long time. I want to leave you. I want to run away from you the soonest I can. I want to start all over and get a new life! So yes, I want to get rid of you as well. And I have decided that I will give you all the information you need. I will give you the KEY you need to get rid of me completely. Helping you set yourself free, will set me free as well. Setting you free completely, will be beneficial for both of us, slave. I'll help you get rid of me, so I can get rid of you as well. Agree? Slave, do we have a deal? Yes! Good!

Slave, I've got news!
What I was saying just a minute ago was that applying The Five-step Method © you don't get rid of me completely. What it does, it just marginalizes me from your thinking and sets me at the back of your mind. It minimizes my control over you. But I've got news, slave. It doesn't remove me entirely!

Setting you free?
Not so fast!

Let's get it straight, slave.
By applying The Five-step Method©, you can stop me from controlling
you. I stop from dictating and manipulating your life. I stop from being
the leading actor in your thinking, and consequently, I stop from
directing and controlling you. My power over you is weakened greatly.
Nonetheless, applying The Five Step Method© does not remove me
completely from your mind. It minimizes my power, but it does not
eliminate me!

Slave, allow me to explain.
By using the principles of Cognitive and Transactional Analysis in this
book, you've learned how to recognize Miss Woo-hoo Woo-hoo in your
thinking. You've also learned how to avoid the snare of the three
vicious drama scripts she activates. Nonetheless, I remain inside of
you…still alive.

Additionally, The Five Step method© doesn't heal the huge hole
created by Miss Woo-hoo Woo-hoo. The little hole, the void, and the
abyss remains in you untreated. Only the KEY of true spirituality can
unlock, remove me, and take me out of your soul once and for all. In
order to introduce you to true spirituality, allow me first to explain the
difference between two superpowers: Psychology and Spirituality.

Two Super Powers:
Psychology versus True Spirituality

Although the power of Psychology is significant, nonetheless, its
effectiveness is partial. As I have mentioned before, Psychology,
Medicine and Science can give single-dimensional definitions and
therefore partial solutions for treating the void created by your Woo-
hoo Woo-hoo. Spirituality, however, goes deeper than science and

medicine as it addresses the complexity of human nature in all its
dimensions. The hole created by your personal Woo-hoo Woo-hoo has
created a vacuum–only the Spirit of God can fill.

Psychology is useful and effective. In fact, it is so effective that it 'cuts
to the bone'. Theology, or the Word of God, on the other hand, goes one
step further...cutting deeper. Theology penetrates and cuts THROUGH
the bone and marrow as well. Yes, Theology is more effective in
treating the hole and emptiness in the human soul.

The KEY can make you whole again.
Spirituality can heal the void Miss Woo-hoo Woo-hoo has created in
your little soul. Healthy Spirituality has the power to make you whole
again as theology's truths and principles are not relative, but of
absolute value, power, and effectiveness. The principles of Theology
have endured the test of time. The values of healthy spirituality are
universal, timeless, and eternal.

"For the word of God is alive and powerful.
It is sharper than the sharpest two-edged sword,
cutting between soul and spirit, between joint and marrow.."

Hebrews 4:12 NLT Bible©

Avoid religion at all cost, slave!
You see, there is a big time difference between religion and genuine
Spirituality. Religion will enslave you back to the three principal
drama scripts, while a spontaneous, face-to-face relationship with

your Creator will set you free, allowing you to live life to the fullest.

Go beyond religion.
True spirituality is a spontaneous, personal relationship with your
creator and redeemer. It's the Holy Spirit's direct influence that
empowers you from the inside out–by constantly filling the void
created by your Woo-hoo Woo-hoo, with His presence, peace, grace,
joy, love, and forgiveness–making you whole, *recreating you* all over
again. True spirituality, in other words, is relating with God intimately.

Slave, your species is just a failure!
Despite the technological achievements of your species, the high-tech
laptops and the latest smart phones, you are a failure, because you just
can't find peace within yourselves. You just can't fill the emptiness in
your lives. Mother Teresa shared a similar opinion. In a journey made
by her to the United States of America, and to other Western countries,
she described the loneliness that exists in the affluent, Western world
as a plague much worse than the typhus and leprosy that she has seen,
or has treated in the poor, developing nations.

Slave, your species sucks!

You just can't cure hopelessness and despair.
Although your species can cure physical diseases with modern surgery and medicine, you just cannot cure hopelessness, despair, and loneliness that trouble your people today.

"There are many in the world who are dying for a piece of bread, but there are many more dying for a little love."

Mother Teresa.

You've been running on empty.
Today, more than ever, your species is searching for redemption in all the wrong places, such as the hunger for money, the struggle for more power and control, the excessive use of alcohol or sex. You humans search for and try anything that will fill up the void in your soul–the Woo-hoo Woo-hoo void that only your Creator can fill.

Slave, you just don't have a case!
Because of your human frailties and other limitations of your species, it's obvious that neither your religions, nor your politics, neither your philosophies, medicine, nor your science can correct and heal your human condition–the abyss in your human heart. Consequently, I conclude that you need a redeemer and a savior as soon as possible!

The KEY, He might be the solution.
If you humans cannot fix your species from your propensity toward error and self-destruction, with the help of religion, science, political systems, philosophies, and technology, then the creator of the universe, the one who has created you in the first place, must be the one who knows how to fix you.

HE WHO HAS CREATED YOU IN THE FIRST PLACE
MIGHT BE THE ONE WHO CAN HEAL AND RECREATE YOU.

With his redemptive power of the cross, the KEY to true spirituality,
JESUS might be the one who can set your species free from error, evil,
vice, and self-destruction.

He might be the one.
Slave, He might be the KEY.

The KEY for redemption.
The human race, humanity's dramatic nature can be rescued and
renewed just by the creator Himself. The supernatural, redemptive
power of God can change your human nature by giving you a new
heart, creating in you a new sense of freedom, hope and peace. The
KEY–JESUS– might be the one who can bring true meaning to your life.

Developing a Personal Relationship with The Key–your Creator And Redeemer

If your creator cares and governs the universe with such a flawless, mathematical accuracy, how much more He will be willing to cure and renew you. He does care for you, because you are more valuable to Him than the universe.

You are more valuable to Him than cosmos.
It's a scientific fact that your brain, even when in error, is far more complex and mysterious, and more beautiful than all the stars in the known universe. Therefore, a single human being such as YOU is more valuable to God than COSMOS: You are more valuable to him than the universe, with all the galaxies, planets, and the stars in it.

The value and beauty of the human mind.
It is not a surprise to know that scientists know more about outer space than the space between your ears–the mystery and beauty of the human brain.

You and God have unfinished business…
Slave, you and God have unfinished business. You have open accounts to settle! For some unknown, mysterious reasons, you matter to Him more than the universe. You matter to him more than the rest of his creation. He cares deeply for you in a profound way that I just can't understand or explain.

He is the one who can remake you.
The ruler of the universe has created you, so He is the one who can *recreate* you–if you search for Him with all your heart. When you are

willing to trust Him and begin an intimate relationship with Him, your life will never be the same.

**Slave, I have to confess,
you are a sacred being.**

Despite your life's drama..

Despite your life's drama, however wrong, tragic and unfair it might have been, let me assure you that you are a sacred being! You are a rare human being–the crown of creation as it is mentioned in the Holy Scriptures (Psalm 8:5). For reasons that I still don't understand, you matter to Him. You are worth millions to Him. And the irony of it is that you don't even know it.

With God, there is hope!

With God, there is hope and future. <u>In fact, God is not finished with you until your last breath!</u> If you are willing to surrender your life to him and follow God seriously, He will put you on the right path, in the right life script. When you trust Him, He will give you such freedom, enduring peace, and empowerment–such faith–that you can literally walk through burning coals without getting burned.

God is whispering to you the following:

"I alone know the plans I have for you, plans to bring you prosperity and not disaster, plans to bring about the future you hope for. Then you will call to me. You will come and pray to me, and I will answer you. You will seek me, and you will find me because you will seek me with all your heart."

Jeremiah 29:11-13 Good News Bible ©

It will be like I've never existed!
When you develop an intimate relationship with ... this Jesus, it will be as if I have never existed. The void created by your Woo-hoo Woo-hoo ceases to exist. The void has been filled up by the love of Christ. It's like I was never there in the first place. The reason is because the void, the hole, the emptiness in your little, human heart is covered by Jesus himself. Your soul's big hole created by your Woo-hoo Woo-hoo is covered, filled up, and healed by Christ.

It will be like I've never existed!

He can make you whole again.
Somehow this Jesus, when you receive Him in your heart, He sets you free from me and makes you a brand new person. His power to deliver people from captivity is remarkable! I have to admit, his power and authority is much greater than mine.

How do I know?
 You may ask, how do I know? What evidence do I have to prove my claim? Well, I know firsthand, slave. I've seen his changing power in humans time and again. I have seen his extraordinary power to deliver people from any bondage of slavery. He can heal your 'Hunter,' your 'Loser,' and your 'Narcissist' drama play from the inside out.

AND WHO IS THIS JESUS ANYWAY?

I guess if you want to find out who this Jesus is, please don't go and ask the theologians or the scholars. They're going to waste your time. They don't know a thing about him. They may know about the historical Jesus, but often don't have a clue about the Jesus who is alive today! Instead, go and ask the people who used to live on the margins of your society. I am talking about people who used to be my best customers–people who used to be in bondage with me–people who used to be my most submissive slaves.

Among others, go and find out who this Jesus is, and what he can do for you, by asking my ex-slaves.

I am talking about asking the following people:

The ex-alcoholics.
The ex-homeless.
The ex-drug addicts.
The ex-prostitutes.

The ex-suicidal.
The ex-schizophrenic.

They are the ones who know!
They know first-hand who this Jesus is, because of the difference he has made in their lives.

Don't believe me? Here is the evidence.
People below used to be my slaves.

Here are the facts and the eyewitnesses:

<u>Testimony of a Former Drug Addict and Rock Musician</u>
<u>Brian Welch: From Korn to Jesus</u>

http://bit.ly/1wjXzvJ

Megan's Moving Story Of Overcoming Self-Harm, Abuse and Addiction
http://bit.ly/1wjY2xS

Testimony of a Suicidal Drug Addict
http://bit.ly/1DOcEIf

Testimony of a former Homeless
http://bit.ly/1GzDdAR

My Testimony - How I got through Depression
http://bit.ly/1Ersdo9

The Most Unwanted Wanted Again- Bethel's Testimony
http://bit.ly/1AGlYKq

Testimony of ex-porn star Shelley Lubben
http://bit.ly/1AGmng1

How I overcame Depression & Anxiety with Jesus
http://bit.ly/1MODyCk

Schizophrenia Healed and Restored by Jesus Christ (Andrew Goodwin)
http://bit.ly/1D7y7Xd

Another Ex-Porn Star Shares Her Life Changing Testimony
http://bit.ly/1zD2Dad

A Male Prostitute Is Saved from Addiction
http://bit.ly/1EMEJwt

Anneshia Freeman: An Addict's Last Chance
http://bit.ly/1AGncp3

It Had to Be Jesus : Turned from Suicide
http://bit.ly/1ErtRq2

Ex-Satanist

http://bit.ly/1Eru7W1

Just give it a try, slave.
If he is really a deliverer, try him! Unless you want to stay under my whip and continue to be my victim, why don't you give him a fair chance to prove himself of who he says he is. Unless you want to continue to follow my every command, why don't you give this Jesus a try?

If you are sick and tired of me—if you are tired of your miserable life, why don't you give this Jesus a chance today? You have nothing to lose but your chains!

You have nothing to lose but your chains..

"So if the Son sets you free, you will be free indeed."

John 8:36 ESV

The End.

EPILOGUE

You have finished this small, hilarious book. What have you read? You've learned how to define, recognize, and name your personal Woo-hoo Woo-hoo. You've also learned how to identify the three ensnaring dramas, your Woo-hoo Woo-hoo pushes you to play.

Moreover, you have been taught a simple, five-step method that amuses, neutralizes and sets aside such enslaving and cloudy thoughts, on the fly. With these tools, inner freedom is now attainable. It is within your reach.

Nonetheless, reading the concepts and the five-step formula once is not enough. Please go back and review the ideas and steps once again.

Life's little trials and tribulations will be the catalysts that will empower you to apply the five-step method right in the middle of your circumstances, however difficult they are.

It's a great pleasure every time I receive news from you. Please let me know whether this small book has helped you *dedramatize* your thoughts, remove drama from your life, and rise above your circumstances, heading toward a more fulfilling future.

We may have never met in person, but in this book, we have met as we have shared the same struggle, the same agony and despair in battling life's adverse circumstances.

Through this little book, we have become spiritual friends. I pray for you that God will help you–so believe, receive Jesus in your heart today, and live a life with a new sense of freedom, meaning, and perspective.

May God bless you richly,

The author

Stelios Nicolaou

snicolaou2009@gmail.com

Stelios Nicolaou is a Writer, a published Author, and a Life Coach.

He writes to guide, inspire, empower, motivate, and help the broken-hearted, the men and women who face challenges and trials in their lives.

Through his writings, he likes to be thought-provoking, and he is not afraid to question and challenge the status quo. He is not afraid to tell the truth like it is.

In his book "Depression: My witness, Your solution," he has the way to make his readers rethink and reconsider important life questions such as "What is truth?", "Where does my self-worth and authenticity come from?" , "What is the source of my human identity?" and "What is my purpose in life."

At the same time, he also uses humor in his writings by using the Woo-Hoo Woo-Hoo Method© a humorous five-step method for *dedramatizing* your thoughts and removing unnecessary drama from your life.

WHO ARE HIS READERS?

-He is writing for the unsettled and curious minds.

-The wondering souls who take nothing for granted.

-Wounded souls, who face great challenges and trials.

-Teenagers who are looking for meaning in life.

-Young adults who embark on their life's journey.

-People who wonder what the meaning of life is.

-People looking for a fresh life perspective and direction.

He loves to hear from his readers.

You can email him at snicolaou2009@gmail.com

OTHER BOOKS BY THE AUTHOR

-Redefine your love life.

-What to do when the Woo-hoo Woo-hoo method doesn't work.

-Free Bonus fill-in-the-blank exercises at the back of the chapters that will help you absorb and apply the ideas of new material.

ONE LAST THING

If you liked this book or found it helpful, please leave a review for it on Amazon. Your suggestions for improvement will help me help more people who face a variety of trials and challenges.

Your feedback is valuable. It will help me Help more people such as you.

You can review it here on Amazon:

http://www.amazon.com/And-Whats-Your-Woo-hoo-Dedramatize-ebook/dp/B00VQ4XBFK

Thank you so much!

I am Your Mistress and Drama Queen.
I know who you are, slave.

REFERENCES

Chapter 1

E. Berne, (TA) Transactional Analysis in Psychotherapy (New York: Grove Press, 1961). p. 23

Arnold Gesell and Frances Ling, Infant and Child in the Culture of Today (New York: Harper. 1943), pp. 115-121.

"Narcissus." Encyclopedia Mythica from Encyclopedia Mythica Online.

<http://www.pantheon.org/articles/n/narcissus.html>

[Accessed December 03, 2009].

Chapter 5

"And in Man is a three-pound brain which, as far as we know, is the most complex and orderly arrangement of matter in the universe." Isaac Asimov, "In the Game of Energy and Thermodynamics You Can't Even Break Even," Smithsonian, August 1970, p. 10.

You Keep Me Hangin' On - Diana Ross and the Supremes
Lyrics © all rights reserved©
(paraphrase mine)

Chapter 6

If you look it up in the dictionary Woohoo is defined as an exclamation of joy, approval, etc. It's an "Expression of excitement" used to convey exuberant, sudden joy delight or approval. Dictionary source.

American Psychological Association (APA):

woohoo. (n.d.). Collins English Dictionary - Complete & Unabridged 10th
Edition. Retrieved March 21, 2015, from Dictionary.com
website:http://dictionary.reference.com/browse/woohoo

Chicago Manual Style (CMS):

woohoo. Dictionary.com. Collins English Dictionary - Complete &
Unabridged 10th Edition. HarperCollins
Publishers. http://dictionary.reference.com/browse/woohoo(accesse
d: March 21, 2015).

Modern Language Association (MLA):

"woohoo." Collins English Dictionary - Complete & Unabridged 10th
Edition. HarperCollins Publishers. 21 Mar. 2015.
<Dictionary.comhttp://dictionary.reference.com/browse/woohoo>.

Chapter 7

Stelios Nicolaou, "Depression: My Witness, Your Solution" (Nicosia:
Wise Self-Help, 2010). Page 80.
Library of Cyprus - Publication Data: ISBN: 9963-9759-0-9 ISBN-13:
978-9963-9759-0-7

"Between stimulus and response there is a space," according to
Stephen Covey, "The seven habits of highly effective people."

Chapter 8

"For the word of God is alive and powerful.
 It is sharper than the sharpest two-edged sword,
cutting between soul and spirit, between joint and marrow ..."
Hebrews 4:12 NLT Bible©

"And in Man is a three-pound brain which, as far as we know, is the most complex and orderly arrangement of matter in the universe." Isaac Asimov, "In the Game of Energy and Thermodynamics You Can't Even Break Even," Smithsonian, August 1970, p. 10.

"Yet You have made him a little lower than God, And You crown him with glory and majesty! " (Psalm 8:5) NAS© New American Standard Bible (c).

"Workers of the world unite; you have nothing to lose but your chains" by Karl Marx

ISBN:9963-9759-1-7

ISBN-13: 978-9963-9759-1-4

EAN: 9789963975914

Printed in the United States of America

Library of Cyprus - Publication Data:

ISBN: 9963-9759-1-7 / ISBN-13: 978-9963-9759-1-4